# Barnard Castle

## in old picture postcards

by
Alan Wilkinson

Second edition

European Library - Zaltbommel/Netherlands MCMLXXXV

GB   ISBN 90 288 2304 2 / CIP

*European Library in Zaltbommel/Netherlands publishes among other things the following series:*

**IN OLD PICTURE POSTCARDS** *is a series of books which sets out to show what a particular place looked like and what life was like in Victorian and Edwardian times. A book about virtually every town in the United Kingdom is to be published in this series. By the end of this year about 175 different volumes will have appeared. 1,250 books have already been published devoted to the Netherlands with the title* **In oude ansichten.** *In Germany, Austria and Switzerland 500, 60 and 15 books have been published as* **In alten Ansichten;** *in France by the name* **En cartes postales anciennes** *and in Belgium as* **En cartes postales anciennes** *and/or* **In oude prentkaarten** *150 respectively 400 volumes have been published.*

*For further particulars about published or forthcoming books, apply to your bookseller or direct to the publisher.*

*This edition has been printed and bound by Grafisch Bedrijf De Steigerpoort in Zaltbommel/Netherlands.*

# INTRODUCTION

The small country town of Barnard Castle has had many functions in its long history. Though weapons and flint tools found in the vicinity indicate that man was living there some three or four thousand years ago, the visible history of the town begins at the time of the Roman occupation.

The Roman road from the village of Bowes, four miles south, is part of a continuous straight line which runs the full length of Galgate, one of Barnard Castle's main streets, before becoming lost in the countryside – though after a further fifteen miles it reappears to form the main street of Bishop Auckland. This road crossed the River Tees, and it was near the site of the ford that Barnard Castle was built.

In its upper reaches the River Tees is a turbulent river; it becomes wider and calmer as it leaves the Pennines behind and eventually forms a navigable channel as it nears the North Sea. Approximately midway between its source and its mouth, Barnard Castle is situated where the Tees is still swift-flowing, but where deep pools alternate with shallow stretches. It was at one such place that the Romans forded the river, and the name of the nearby village of Startforth (Ford on the Road) suggests that the site continued to be used after the Romans had gone.

Nearby, some hundred and fifty yards downstream, the northern bank rises in a rocky outcrop to a height of over seventy feet above the river. It is a perfect position for a stronghold, and that is where Bernard Baliol, a member of a family which came from France after the Norman Conquest, built his castle – Bernard's Castle – and round it grew the town which still bears a variant of its name.

The river had its part to play in civil as well as military life, for it was the source of power for the Lord's mill which ground the villagers' corn – in return for a payment of one sixteenth of the total produce – and a water mill (now disused) stands on the same site today.

During the Middle Ages manufacturing combined with agriculture, and by the seventeenth century Barnard Castle had become an industrial centre concentrating on woollen and leather goods. Wool continued to be the basis of eighteenth century industry, when the river was again important, not just for driving the machinery by a succession of weirs, sluices and water-wheels, but also as a highly regarded medium for the use of dyes.

Even when steam power was introduced, the riverside mills were still used. Barnard Castle became quite famous for its carpets, and its shoe thread was widely exported. Tanning continued and also the production of hemp ropes for a variety of uses. Unfortunately the success of the riverside industries led to great overcrowding and insanitary conditions in the houses that huddled together between the castle cliff and the mills, and in 1849 there was a dreadful outbreak of Asiatic Cholera. Good came out of evil when, following an official enquiry, a report was issued which led to the establishment of a Local Board of Health, later the Urban District Council.

Throughout the period of this industrial development near the river, Barnard Castle was fulfilling its other function of being a market town for the surrounding agricultural area. This feature of the town took place in spacious streets well above the river level. Livestock and farm produce were sold in specified areas, and a mixed market was held on the cobbled areas in the Market Place and extended part of the way down The Bank. Today the livestock sales are in a different part of the town, but the general market continues on a smaller scale in the traditional area.

An Elizabethan stone bridge had ensured that Barnard Castle

maintained its significance as a river crossing, but in the last hundred and fifty years the town has tended to develop away from the river, as the old buildings in that area grew less acceptable for dwelling or industry. Foundries and factories were built on the higher land, and the railway and modern roads simplified and speeded the movement of materials and finished products.

In the 1930's Barnard Castle was again exporting goods, but this time it was road signs and road-cleaning equipment, and a decade later a factory belonging to a large pharmaceutical firm with world-wide connections was established in the town. Reviving a traditional industry, a leather factory opened in a riverside building, and more recently another firm dealing in leather goods has been developed.

A more surprising addition to Barnard Castle's significance took place in the nineteenth century in the form of The Bowes Museum, a magnificent and ornate building housing a valuable and diverse collection of artistic treasures as well as displays on aspects of local history. Originally privately built, it is now administered by Durham County Council, and attracts thousands of visitors each year.

During the Second World War a very old function of the town was revived – it again became a military centre. It had long had connections with the Durham Light Infantry because the Earl of Darlington raised the Durham Militia at Barnard Castle in 1759 and the town became the Headquarters of the 3rd Battalion, Durham Light Infantry; in the 1940's it found itself surrounded by military camps housing a variety of regiments, but chiefly the Royal Armoured Corps. To concentrate on the town's industrial or military role would, however, give an inaccurate picture of Barnard Castle. It retains the essential quality of a market town, still showing clear indications of its history, and set in rich and varied scenery. This is its abiding charm, a town of character having woods, fields, rivers and streams as its immediate surroundings, with moorland hills beyond; it is these qualities that are enjoyed by its five thousand inhabitants, and which increasingly attract tourists and holiday makers to Barnard Castle and its surrounding district of Teesdale.

*Acknowledgements:*
Copyright photographs, as listed, have been reproduced by permission of
Beamish North of England Open Air Museum, Stanley, Co. Durham (Nos. 17, 30, 31, 48, 61).
The Bowes Museum, Barnard Castle, Co. Durham (Nos. 15, 16, 27, 47, 69, 70).
The D.L.I. Museum, Aykley Heads, Durham (Nos. 2, 3, 7, 8, 36, 60, 63).
Mr. H.C. Casserley, Berkhamsted, Herts. (No. 4).

Thanks are also due to the following for kindly supplying photographs and useful information:
Mr. and Mrs. G. Barker, Mr. F.V. Deacon, Mr. A.R. Farrar, Mrs. J. Lee, Mr. A. Maude, Mr. S. Maude, Mr. and Mrs. O. McKitton, Mrs. E. Nichols, Mr. E. Scott, Mr. S.D. Shannon, Mr. W. Taylor, Alderman R. Watson, Colonel W.I. Watson, Mr. C. Woodhams, Mrs. T.M. Wright, Barnard Castle Cricket Club and Barnard Castle School.

Practical help from the following is gratefully acknowledged:
Mr. G.H. Charlesworth, Mr. A. Maude, Mr. P. Robinson, Mr. J. McTaggart, Mr. Andrew Wilkinson and Mrs. Jean Wilkinson.

30678 BARNARD CASTLE, GALGATE WEST.

1. Barnard Castle was never a walled town, but five of the entrances to the town have the word 'gate' (meaning 'way') in their names. Galgate leads into the town from the north. In the 1880's the Local Board of Health was much concerned with making it a more dignified approach to the town, especially since this was the first street seen by visitors who had come by train. The picture shows how well they succeeded. (The iron railings enclosing trees, lawns and flower-beds were removed during the Second World War.) Across the valley can be seen the Roman road, on a section of which Galgate stands. To the left is a postman, in his tall peaked cap; the laden horse-drawn carts are probably conveying coal from the railway goods yard; in front of the corner-shop with its adjacent public house stands a railwayman – a reminder that Montalbo Terrace (to the right) led to the passenger station.

2. Considering its importance to the town, the railway station was little photographed – until the departure of the 17th Battalion, Durham Light Infantry in 1915. The gabled frontage gives an indication of the size of the station buildings, but the platform extended at each end well beyond the limit of the roofs. The line from Darlington to Barnard Castle opened in 1856 with a terminus in what is now Montalbo Road; in 1861 that station became the goods station, and a new passenger station was opened. The lines to Kirkby Stephen and to Bishop Auckland closed in 1962; Middleton-in-Teesdale to Darlington via Barnard Castle closed to passengers in 1964 and to goods trains in 1965. The passenger station area is now the site of a large car park for employees of a nearby factory.

Text visible in photograph:
GOOD LUCK
TO THE
17TH DLI
BARNARD CASTLE
SEP 24th 1915
13

3. The main part of the station's buildings forms the background of this emotional scene. A contemporary account says that 'the interest was deep and heartfelt for there was the touching memory that they were all somebody's relatives'. There had been various sing-songs the night before and a farewell supper. The War Emergency Committee presented each man with a campaign wallet and a parcel of sandwiches. Many other gifts were passed to the men when they were in the carriages. As the special trains, drawn by main-line engines, set off 'a mighty roar resounded into the station rafters'. Many people also assembled at the Harmire Crossing to cheer the soldiers as the trains passed.

4. This picture is taken from the same position as the previous one, but on a quieter (and later) occasion, and looking east, instead of west. An ex-Great Northern Railway 4-4-0 NO. 4354 arrives with a train from Darlington. It was not a popular class of locomotive with enginemen and when used on the Stainmore Line had to have a modified cab to give more protection against the weather. Nearby wagons are from the London Midland and Scottish Railway and the Southern Railway. The signal cabin beside the Harmire Level Crossing is visible in the background. Near it a branch line ran to the goods sidings in Montalbo Terrace. It crossed the minor road as a single line without any gates or warning signs. Hidden by the trucks and guard's van were two engine sheds and a turntable.

5. Several hotels provided horse-drawn conveyances to meet visitors at the railway station; perhaps this is one of them coming down Galgate on a winter morning. Only the centre of the street was made up into a road, though a gutter had been constructed at the foot of the slope to the left. In 1882 a resident who was charged with 'placing rubbish or offensive matter on the highway' claimed that less than half the width of the street was highway, and added that he had been really laying stones on part of the other area to improve 'what in wet weather is a complete bog'. He thought the wide area might be regarded as a village green or common, for he remembered boys playing cricket on it. At about the same period a touring circus also performed there!

6. At the turn of the century holiday-makers as well as townsfolk regarded Galgate as one of the town's 'promenades'. In addition to enclosures at the upper end, there was an avenue of trees at the lower part of the road, and the impressive Methodist Church, with seating for 620, was erected in 1894. The drinking fountain, designed to serve man and beast, had been built in 1874, and can just be seen through the trees on the left. The road sweepers have been at work already, but otherwise there are few people about in this early morning scene; the two horses are chained together thus needing only one carter for the two vehicles – and he is smoking his pipe at ease in one of the carts.

7. Galgate was improved by having a stepped pavement on the north side and here it forms a grandstand for spectators of 'Trooping the Colours' on 9th July, 1914. The old colours of the 4th Durham Light Infantry were going to be 'laid-up' in the Parish Church. Behind the old colours are the new ones, presented at Deerbolt Camp in 1906 by the Earl of Durham. (They, too, are now in the Parish Church.) A bugle band further enhanced the proceedings; all participants were in red tunics with green cuffs and collars. This and other pictures of the occasion give a clear impression of a hot summer day of the period, with the ladies in white blouses and carrying sunshades, and the gentlemen wearing round straw hats.

8. In June, 1913, Pt. R.E. Smith of West Hartlepool was drowned while bathing in a deep section of the Tees known as 'Gentlemen's Hole' (more recently shortened to 'the Gents'), which was not an authorised military bathing place. He had been at the annual training camp at Deerbolt as a member of the 3rd Bn. Durham Light Infantry Special Reserves. A knell was rung from the Parish Church, and a military funeral followed an inquest at which the coroner recommended the erection of warning notices on each bank of the fatal place. The cortege has turned out of Galgate into King Street on its way to the Church cemetery where three volleys were fired over the grave and the Last Post was sounded. King Street has not visibly changed much since this sad occasion, except that a tree can be seen above the wall on a site where the Teesdale District Council Chamber now stands.

9. The roof-line of this side of Galgate (circa 1900) has changed little, and the replacement of stone slabs with slates had already begun to alter the character of the roofs themselves. The main alteration has been the introduction of modern shop fronts, replacing others that represented modernisation in their own day. One building (just above the horse's collar) altered its frontage to become the entrance to the Scala Cinema, one of three in the town in 1929 when it advertised as 'one of the prettiest cinemas for miles around' and the 'Premier Picture House'. It had its own orchestra, and the entrance was dignified with two Doric columns, still in position. Sir Roderick Murchison, a former President of the Royal Geographical Society, once lived in the impressive three-storey house. The house beyond it has been demolished to make an entry to a large car park.

10. Abraham Hilton, seen here on a pony in lower Galgate, died on 1st October, 1902, aged 87. His name survives in the Hilton Charities, the original terms of which show the founder's kindly and understanding nature: recipients were to be old, afflicted or infirm — and such as were not likely to apply for Parish relief. By 1913 there were a hundred annuitants. One of his dying requests was that his ponies should be treated as pensioners. Born in a thatched cottage in Bridgegate, Mr. Hilton became a Tea and Spirit Merchant living at 33 Galgate. He is buried, at his own request, in a rural setting above the river near Cotherstone; he loved natural scenes, believed in God, revered the teaching of Christ, but did not accept all the doctrines of any religious sect, so felt he should not be interred within one of their burial grounds.

11. Barnard Castle's market area extended in a continuous line from Galgate to below the so-called Market Cross or Butter Market. Sheep, pigs and cattle were sold at the widest part of Galgate. A stone near the present entrance to the car park marked the boundary of the market. It was also the area used on Hirings Day when farm-hands sought new jobs and farmers looked for new workers for the coming year. The large house in the photograph is today's Post Office; its small front and side garden has gone but its basic structure is unchanged. In 1884 it was the residence of Surgeon Munroe of the Durham Militia. Beyond it is a clear view into Yorkshire (as it then was) which has since been obscured by the trees in Woodleigh garden whose boundary wall can be seen on the picture; the footpath beside it was called Flatts Lane.

12. Barnard Castle Cricket Club was founded in 1832 and has been in continuous existence ever since. Its first ground was outside the town at Woolhouse Farm, and the club moved to the Baliol Street ground (off Galgate) in the 1870's. The picture shows the club's team (augmented by guest players) for a match against Mr. R. Healey's Darlington XI in 1929. Left to right (standing): R. Watson, H.F. Finlay, M. Adlard, Col. R.C. Grellet (Captain), A. Waine, F.E. Baker (Barnard Castle School's Professional), J.T. Winter and G. Duffy (umpire). Seated: N. Harper (Bishop Auckland), S. Snowden (Hutton Rudby), C.E. Charlton (Bishop Auckland) and H. Lamb (scorer). The club's regular 1st XI that year played 26 matches, won 10, lost 11, and drew 5. Colonel Grellet, a forceful captain, was top of both the batting and bowling averages, scoring an average of 21 runs in 19 completed innings, and taking 70 wickets at an average of 9.1 runs per wicket.

13. In the middle years of its long history the Cricket Club incorporated a Lawn Tennis section, with grass courts inside the southern boundary of the cricket area. When the cricket 1st XI was at home, the tennis nets and the back-netting at each end of the courts were removed, but the 2nd XI and the tennis players shared the arena. Though the field is called the Baliol Street Ground, it is actually entered from Marshall Street (seen in the background). The former street is shown on the 1859 Ordnance Survey Map as already one-third built, whereas Marshall Street was not completed and paved until the 1880's, when the cricket ground had already been established. The tennis pavilion 'doubled' as the cricketers' tea-hut, their pavilion being at the other end of the ground. The tennis pavilion (shown here) was replaced in 1929 by another which has since given way to a commodious club house.

14. At Whitsuntide in the 1880's Athletic and Cycling races were held on the Cricket Field. In 1885 a group of cyclists rode from the Tyne to the Tees, and decided to make it an annual outing when they discovered such activities as the sports ready-made for them to join in. Soon a Cyclists Meet Committee helped to organise the sports, and racing celebrities competed in them, though there were more light-hearted events, too. This card is dated 1915 when the war no doubt accounts for a relatively sparse crowd. In 1893, admittedly a bumper year, six thousand people had watched the sports. In the distance can be seen Woolhouse Farm where the Cricket Club had its first ground when it was founded.

15. As the Whitsuntide Cyclists Meet became established, it acquired features which became traditional. One of these was the Whit Monday fancy dress procession which began in the 1890's. In this picture, taken in 1911, it is passing through lower Galgate on its way to be judged in the Castle Garth, which was reached through the yard of the King's Head Hotel. That year's procession was watched by at least ten thousand people lining the streets. It was said to contain elements that were 'burlesque, frivolous and educational' — it included John Bull and Britannia, and Tired Tim, and Sir Walter Scott's poem 'Rokeby' was depicted, in sixteenth century costume. Here it is passing another traditional feature, the travelling fair which annually occupied lower Galgate at Whitsuntide. It, like the procession, has continued to the present day, but now it occupies the town's car park at Spring Bank Holiday.

16. It is now ninety years since anybody saw this scene. It is the house and side-entry known as Bland's Yard which was demolished to make way for the Methodist Church at the foot of Galgate. The four houses that formerly occupied the site of the church were typical of the streets of many villages or small towns, and the dominant building which replaced them made a great difference to the appearance of the town. The yards or gardens behind the houses enjoyed a more open situation than most of the town's yards, which were generally far from healthy. The Scar Top, which lies beyond, was a rough patch of ground and for a long time was used as a caravan-park by the owners of the attractions of the Galgate fair at Whitsuntide.

17. Mr. J.G. Johnson (butcher) acquired the corner property in 1870 and rebuilt it as it stands today; below its shop window a pretty picture of the castle is incorporated in the arrangement of tiles which has survived several changes of ownership. Shrubs in the little garden of what is now the Post Office and trees in Woodleigh garden frame a busy yet peaceful scene on a sunny summer afternoon circa 1917. Bicycles, perambulators, a hand-cart and two horse-drawn vehicles present little danger to children who dawdle in the roadway. The rather ornate cart on the left may be selling ice-cream; the distant one is heavily laden with hay. It turns into the Market Place, leaving in its wake a workman dealing with some aspect of the road's surface.

18. Three successive pictures illustrate aspects of Barnard Castle's celebration of the Coronation of King George V and Queen Mary on 22nd June, 1911. The boys of the North Eastern County School were responsible for the 'floriated arch' erected between Mr. Johnson's shop and Mrs. Carter's residence at the junction of Horse Market and Galgate. In the distance a flag flies above the Witham Hall where the decorations were organised by the County School's Art Master, Mr. Parkinson. 'The Teesdale Mercury' commended his choice of 'chaste colouring'. Other features of the town's decorations included the use of shields and a metallic crown with perforations in the design through which gas jets were fixed and lit up at night.

19. Mr. William Smith, Chairman of the Urban District Council, stands in the centre of this group (in light suit and hat) in front of the Conservative Club in Horse Market. The decorations had been designed by Mr. Surtees, an architect, and created by the combined efforts of the Women's Unionist Association and the Conservative Club. The white letters on a red background were made at Messrs. William Smith and Sons' works. The building had at one time been the town's Post Office, and is now the D.L.I. Club; though two shops now occupy the ground floor, the doorway and pediment still survive.

20. The Coronation Day's celebrations included peals of bells, a horse parade, a church service, a formal lunch at the Turk's Head, a procession of public organisations and schoolchildren, massed singing led by a choir, which rendered an ode and an anthem under the leadership of Mr. Raper and accompanied by a harmonium on a cart, children's sports on the Demesnes and an old folks' tea. On the following day, 23rd June, about seventy of the organisers, including the schoolteachers, had their own share of the celebrations in the form of an outing in horse-drawn brakes. Their route included Arkengarthdale, Reeth and Richmond, returning by Scotch Corner and Greta Bridge. Grinton Church and Easby Abbey were visited and Mr. Ashby, Vicar of Barnard Castle, explained some frescoe paintings.

21. As the town spread farther from the river, many houses were adapted to become offices or shops. As fashions changed, the shop fronts were altered. When Mr. Ord took over this handsome building, he put his own name over the door before replacing Mr. Dixon's with his own on the wall – but then came the big changes. He removed the ornamental railings over the window. (These were once a feature of shops in the town; now only two remain.) He gave the windows bevelled corners and enlarged them by lowering the sills and removing the Ionic pillars. (A similar pair survives at 2 Market Place.) The windows were re-framed in 'art nouveau' style, and two large lamps were hung in front of them, and can be seen in picture 23. A board over the window stating the owner's name in incised glittering letters completed the modernisa-tion – which has itself been superseded.

22. In 1904 John Harris built two projecting windows onto his shop in Horse Market. The Urban District Council objected that he had occupied part of the public footpath, and took legal action, but the case was dismissed, to applause in court. An appeal was made to the King's Bench which referred the case back to the local magistrates for further information. The case was then argued at a high level, before the Lord Chief Justice announced that the case was again dismissed — with costs against the Council. Early in the affair some jokers trundled a large gun, a Boer War relic, from its usual position in Galgate and pointed it at the offending windows with a placard saying 'Surrender or Die'. Mr. Harris wrote 'No Surrender' on one of his windows — a retort which was well justified by the outcome.

23. This postcard shows a crowded Horse Market at Whitsuntide. A caption reads 'Barney Cycle Meet 1914: Not half dead yet'. This cheerful remark was written because for a few preceeding years it had seemed that the Meet was in decline. Bicycling itself was nationally losing popularity; the Meet of 1910 was officially cancelled through the death of Edward VII; in 1912 there were no sports on the cricket field. The picture shows, however, that the Meet was still a very popular and rather elegant occasion. The men are in suits with flowers in the lapels, and straw boaters and bowler hats almost outnumber caps; a County School boy's cap with radial stripes can be seen near the horse, and the women's hats are resplendent with flowers and ribbons. Within a few weeks many of these men would be in service uniform.

24. Peace at the end of the First World War was officially celebrated on 19th July, 1919. There was a colourful procession, including a tableau of 'Britannia', and various youth and adult groups from local organisations and official bodies such as the Fire Brigade, Police, and Urban District Council, seen here marching along Horse Market after a church service. Captain Higginbotham, who after his military career was school attendance officer for twenty-five years, was Marshall of the procession. An open carriage conveyed three local men who had each lost a leg on active service. The whole procession, led by united choirs, joined in singing the 'Hallelujah Chorus'. Demobilised men were treated to a dinner, and the town's children, headed by a brass band, marched to the Victoria Hall for a film show, and the gift of an orange, buns, and a bag of sweets. The day also included dancing, athletic sports, and fireworks.

25. At first glance it may seem that little has changed since this picture of Horse Market was taken. The curve of the street looks much as it must always have done and the removal of some of the cobbles to create a 'service road' looks modern. However, the 'Yorkshire Penny Bank' has continued its modernisation scheme and the dropping of the word 'Penny' is significant of changed economic conditions. The Star Hotel (formerly 'Goliath's Head') has now gone, its name surviving only in the adjacent Star Yard, and three doors above it the North Eastern Co-operative Society has more recently greatly altered what was W. Hodgson's (later George Burt's) bakery and grocer's shop. Mr. Hodgson also ran the refreshment room at the railway station. The motor-bike leaning against the pleasantly ornamental lamp post – with gas mantle – suggests the changing times.

26. The late afternoon sun reveals that the Market Place has changed in several details since the early years of the century. The cobbles then stretched right up to the lefthand pavement, and at the foot of the slope neatly laid small cobbles formed a gutter. The road itself was not 'made up' but had camber and another gutter. Sun canopies were supported by metal poles inserted into holes in the curbstones, so the cloth stretched across the full width of the pavement. The upper storeys have scarcely changed, but some shop fronts have altered with different owners: older inhabitants will remember Teesdale House (Howson and Reay) next to Hall Street; next was Hall's (or Raine's) chemist's shop; Walter Willson's (with box-shaped sign above the window) announced that they were 'Importers of Foreign Produce', and next door but one was the Joint Stock Bank.

27. Despite arrangements being made to celebrate the coronation of King George V in 1911, one aspect of the situation gave great displeasure to members of the Urban District Council — they had received no instructions to proclaim the King's accession and the Sheriff of Durham had not sent them a copy of the proclamation. They heard that other towns, no more ancient than Barnard Castle, had received a copy; they said that the town had proclaimed monarchs since 1685 — and they decided to go ahead and do so again. So they raised a platform in front of the window of the Council Chamber in the Witham Hall, and on 26th May the church bells rang, a crowd gathered, a fanfare of bugles was sounded, the King was proclaimed (using an earlier form of words), another fanfare was sounded, three cheers were given, the crowd dispersed, and the Council went inside for light refreshments.

Market Place. Barnard Castle.

28. Traditional features of the market are illustrated here: groups of stalls on 'the cobbles', acquaintances meeting from all over the Dale – and difficulties in parking. In this picture, taken before the First World War, the horse-drawn traps are arranged parallel to the curb, with shafts down. Space must have become more limited even by 1920 when a contemporary remembers: *the street-long rows of traps and cape carts backed into the curbing, with their shafts pointing skywards... The farmers and their families, for miles around, would present the shoppers with their delicious farm butter, eggs, fresh vegetables, cream etc. The very air was heavy with the pleasant aroma of butter, cheese, and teacakes, muffins, crumpets, and home-baked bread and the smell of these gastronomic delights mixed with the scent of hay, beer-maltings, harness and horse-flesh.* (H.R. Brown in 'Barnard Castle School, A Centenary Book', 1983.)

BARNARD CASTLE : MARKET PLACE.

29. This view of Market Day was taken from the Butter Market. It shows an apparently random arrangement of stalls, though the carts and traps seem to be more organised. Few horses are visible; the others, released from the shafts, were stabled for the day up the many yards which opened off all the market areas of the town — Lower Galgate, Horse Market and Market Place. Many of the entries can still be seen. The stables were usually associated with public houses, inns and hotels (The Raby Hotel, on the right, is an example) with which the town was plentifully supplied. In the mid-nineteenth century the Market Place, alone, contained The Greyhound, Golden Lion, Half Moon, King's Head, Angel, Rose and Crown, Waterloo, New Waterloo, and Turk's Head — and this is not a complete list.

30. A feature of early North East Cyclists Meets was the decoration of the premises which the various clubs had selected as their headquarters for the occasion. Much effort and artistry went into the activity. The premises illustrated are Milner's Temperance, Waterloo, and Turk's Head Hotels in the Market Place. The decorations on Milner's and the Turk's Head were the respective handiwork of the North Shields' Tyne Cycling Club, and the Brunswick Cycling Club. These were leading clubs in 1909; the former won the prize for the largest attendance (calculated with regard to mileage) in the annual procession through the town; the Brunswickers won the prize for introducing novelty into the procession. There were two processions really: one (on the Saturday night) of clubs which had cycled from their home towns; the other (on Whit Monday) included groups and individuals in fancy dress.

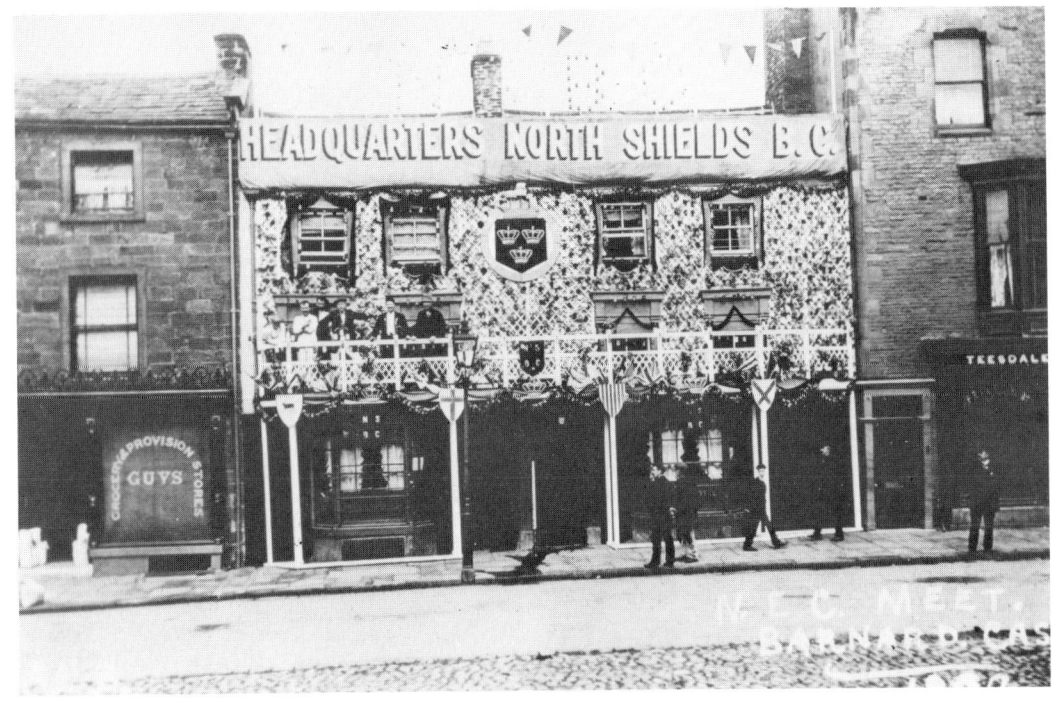

31. The Angel Inn, with its two bay windows, was demolished in the 1930's to make way for a branch of Woolworth's stores, but it is seen here decorated for Whitsuntide, 1909, when it was the headquarters of the whole Meet as well as the North Shields Bicycling Club, which that year won the prize for the club coming the longest distance to ride in the procession. The Angel, like other establishments, advertised throughout the year that it had 'Good accommodation for Cyclists', and many cafes proclaimed 'Cyclists catered for'. In J.B. Priestley's 'The Good Companions' (1929) a proprietor of a café is asked what the difference is between cyclists and other customers. He replies that it is ham, chiefly. 'Cyclists is great on 'am. I've seen the day when one of these cycling clubs would run me right out of 'am by six o'clock Saturday. Mind you, I'm talking about before the war.'

32. This octagonal building has served many purposes; as a Butter Market it accommodated farmers' wives selling dairy produce in the arcade; the room above has been a court-room and the town surveyor's office. As depicted here, the building was the town's fire station, the 'engine' being housed in the central part of the ground floor. Partitions of wood and glass augmented the iron railings already fixed between the outer pillars, and emergency access was gained with a key hanging in a glazed box on the north doors. A fire bell can be seen in the cupola. If the fire was nearby the men pulled the engine themselves; otherwise horses were supplied by the King's Head Hotel. The gable of Amen Corner, beyond, is usefully rather than decoratively employed as an advertisement hoarding.

33. Part of the Fire Brigade poses on the steps on the south side of its 'fire station' in about 1920: F. Metcalfe, H. Culley, A. Blackett, G. Barker; T. Longstaff, R. Hird; J. Miller, T. Chatt, F. Deacon and T. Borrowdale. The log-book for the period tells of fires, monthly drills, and negotiations with the Urban District Council. In 1916 the manual engine was in such poor condition that the men 'respectfully refused to go to country fires' until a thoroughly reliable engine was provided. In 1919 one shilling and sixpence had been paid for attending a fire; after protests the council offered five shillings and sixpence (ten shillings for the captain) for any part of the first three hours at a fire, and one and sixpence per subsequent hour. The council stipulated, however, that the man-power must be cut to twelve. So that the rest could benefit, three men resigned — but two of them gallantly turned out in a voluntary capacity at the next serious fire.

34. Until 1932 these two shops stood, composing Amen Corner, at the junction of The Bank and Newgate. A cobbled way, below Mr. Watson's shop, led to the church. (It has been preserved next to the walled rose-bed that has replaced the shops.) The crowd appears to be watching a military church parade in about 1912. Mr. Finlay catered for man and beast, not only in Provisions, as his windows declare, but with Finlay's oils that eased scalds in people, feloned udders in cows, and broken knees in horses. The right-hand shop was formerly used by Thomas Humphreys, the clockmaker whose name Charles Dickens used in 'Master Humphrey's Clock' (in the course of which he introduced his readers to 'The Old Curiosity Shop' and 'Barnaby Rudge'). Dickens was in Barnard Castle in 1838, when he stayed at the King's Head, while investigating local boarding schools in preparation for writing 'Nicholas Nickleby'. In 1842 Humphreys moved to premises in Market Place, opposite the King's Head.

ST. MARY'S CHURCH, BARNARD CASTLE.

35. The passage of time has obscured much of the Parish Church of St. Mary from this particular viewpoint because of the growth of the trees. The ornamental pinnacles at the east and central levels of the roof have been removed as they became unsafe, but those on the tower remain. The spire on the right belongs to a building variously known as the Free Christian Church or the Unitarian Chapel. It was built in 1870 in memory of George Brown, who had been clerk to the Local Board of Health from 1850 to 1857. It was bought by the Church Council in 1932 to provide recreational facilities for the young men of the Parish Church. It became known as the Institute; Sunday School classes, dances, concerts and plays all took place there. It was demolished to make way for the Parish Hall, the foundation stone of which was laid in 1957.

36. Commanding Officers arrive at the Parish Church for the Laying-up of Colours of the 4th Bn. (Militia) D.L.I. on July 9th, 1914 (not 10th as stated on the photograph). The party has entered through the gateway on the west side of the railings that surrounded the churchyard. The officers, wearing the full dress uniforms of the 4th, 5th, 6th, 7th, 8th and 9th D.L.I., are led by Lord Barnard, Hon. Colonel of the 4th Bn., followed by the High Sheriff of the County. The officer with shoulder belt and tall red plume is Lt. Col. H.C. Watson of Spring Lodge, C.O. 6th Bn. D.L.I. He is wearing the uniform of the King's Royal Rifle Corps, which his battalion always wore. The Vicar is the Reverend H. Bircham and the first hymn was, appropriately, 'Brightly gleams our banner'.

37. The cricket team of the Boys' Department of the Church of England school poses in 1924 with its Headteacher, Mr. F. Wilkinson. When he came to the school in 1922, he introduced organised team games, acquired equipment, and produced cricket and football teams which played against the boys' teams of neighbouring villages, including Bowes, Hutton Magna, and Whorlton. Team: Back row (left to right): Morrell, Robinson, Johnson, unidentified, Walker and Musgrave; Front row: Minnikin, Raine, Deacon, Metcalfe, Coates and Sissons. The schools were at the south-east corner of the churchyard, and as there was no official school playing field, games were played on the Lower Demesnes, nearby, where the children shared the area with grazing animals, men playing quoits, and sometimes a touring circus. Fortunately it was a large area. In 1928 the schools were re-organised into Senior and Junior Mixed Schools.

THE BANK, BARNARD CASTLE.

38. The Bank here has modern pavements with neat high curbs. This improvement has, however, made ramps necessary for hand-carts and horse-drawn vehicles to enter the various yards which opened onto the street. The upper one led to a warehouse, and the other ramp gave access to Broadgates which leads onto the Demesnes. Of the town's five 'gates', Broadgates is the only one with a plural name and is now the narrowest! Perhaps it was broad and had two gates because cattle passed along it for grazing; it also led to two springs, formerly an important part of the water supply to the lower part of the town. The number of shop windows (some of them surviving as house windows) indicates a former high level of population in this area; the road to the Market Place was steep enough for the horses to take a zig-zag route.

39. Described once as 'Barnard Castle's most photographed house', this building has served many purposes in its long history. In Tudor times it must have been a very imposing house, and tradition says that as an inn it accommodated Oliver Cromwell on his over-night stay in the town in October, 1648. It was long known as 'Blagroves' from the name of a former owner, which the present owners believe was an error for 'Blagraves'. At various times it has been — and still is — a restaurant, but other photographs show it as the premises of 'J. Kavanagh (late Brass) Rope Maker' and also a Museum, when its frontage was adorned with a suit of armour and a pair of stocks. The little stone men, representing musicians, are a relatively recent addition, too. In this picture the foot-path and roadside make an attractive pattern of cobbles and flagstones.

40. The Bank was really a continuation of Thorngate, which was itself approached by stepping stones across the river, and so provided an ancient and important entry to the town from the south; the whole street was once known as Thorngate Bank. The narrowness of the entry to Bridgegate (left) is remarkable. Frank Atkinson, a former curator of The Bowes Museum, records that during demolition of a house at the corner, mediaeval timbers were discovered; what had seemed a nineteenth century house was really a much older one 'modernised'. A projecting sign on the right announces 'Wycliffe Cinema'; it was a converted Wesleyan chapel in a yard approached by a covered entry. The area seems to be inhabited entirely by children and idle men in dark suits: perhaps it is Sunday and the children are going to afternoon Sunday School.

41. This is old Bridgegate which has now almost totally disappeared, lawns, trees and a wider road replacing about half of it, with new housing at the east end. Demolition took place just before and after the Second World War. Behind the buildings on the left were riverside mills, and many of the workers lived in and near Bridgegate. The street had contained some dignified eighteenth century houses which became tenements, and other houses crowded up to the castle cliff. The castle can be seen, centre, above the houses. The street supported several public houses and lodging houses, but the financial state of some of the local inhabitants is suggested by the pawnbroker's sign to the right. For a while the street outlived most of the mills that had maintained its crowded existence.

42. This picture gives a clear impression of the way the industrial and domestic buildings crowded together in the narrow space between the cliff and the river, and how one rose above another as they competed for space. On the extreme right a sluice gate can be seen at the entrance to the mill stream which, contained within two strong stone walls, ran to Thorngate Mill, the last of the town's factories to produce woven cloth beside the Tees. During the nineteenth century the town was noted for the production of carpets, blankets, and various garments. As well as powering the mills, the water was highly regarded as a medium for dying. Eventually Durham superseded Barnard Castle as a carpet centre. Other industry in the riverside area included tanneries (continuing a very old tradition) and forges.

43. When steam became harnessed to industrial use, Barnard Castle's water mills were still in sound enough condition to be converted to the new source of power; tall chimneys began to rise among the old buildings, new buildings were created in the traditional industrial area, and the weirs began to disintegrate. The remaining third of the weir at the foot of Thorngate Wynd shows its system of construction with heavy rectangular blocks of stone sloping like a roof on the downstream side. Some were secured with strong iron staples, and massive beams of oak were also bolted to the structure. On the left a new building has risen with its chimney attached, but on the whole the industrial area does not look prosperous.

44. Behind this impressive river frontage lay Bridgegate and its yards and crowded tenements. Approached by narrow passages closed at one end by either the cliff or other buildings, the dwellings were very unhealthy; insanitary conditions were particularly bad between the stone bridge and the Demesnes, but also occurred higher up the town. It was noted that illness repeatedly struck in certain areas, yards, and houses, and in 1849 a particularly severe outbreak of cholera led to a public enquiry and the institution of a Local Board of Health which in 1894 became the Urban District Council. This picture shows that the weirs made the river smooth and deep enough to accommodate small boats conveying cloth to and from the dye pits, some of which were revealed during demolition of the largest building (once Dunn's Carpet Factory) in 1958. Doors opening onto the river also suggest the use of boats.

45. The castle walls supplied many good vantage points for photographers. This view shows the cluster of houses named Bridge End and the open fields close-by which have now disappeared under modern housing. The low whitewashed building across the river was a blacksmith's forge where the traditional articles were made with fire, bellows, and anvil, and where cart-horses were shod. The picture also gives some impression of the west end of Bridgegate and the roofs covered in stone slabs. The houses in the foreground have now gone, but signs of their former existence can still be seen. Though they were tightly packed together, at least some of the houses and factories faced a fresh open countryside, and the clearly-marked field paths show how much these country routes were used.

5721. THE TEES, BARNARD CASTLE.

46. This picture reverses the view of the previous illustration. Standing in the open field, the photographer looks back at the stone bridge over which may just be seen the white cottage which was in the foreground of the other picture. Another white cottage perches high up on the castle cliff. Some of the dwellings used the cliff as their back wall; in at least one case sockets were cut into the natural stone to hold roof timbers. Drifting smoke obscures the houses crowding the hillside. The stone piers on the far side of the river bear a sewage pipe. Cesspools, sometimes centrally placed in communal yards, had been used to take the effluent from shared privies, and other outlets had opened directly onto the river, so a closed pipe was a great mark of progress. Gradually outlets for sewers were created farther downstream, away from the town. The first sewage disposal works were opened in 1894.

47. These buildings are called 'Thorngate Factory' on a mid-nineteenth century map, a name which distinguishes them from Thorngate Mill on the other side of the street. Thorngate Factory, which was entered through an archway opening off the street, was never powered by water, and had a more spacious ground plan than the other woollen factories. (In the present century it has been a leather factory.) The water-front still shows the base of the brick chimney which was demolished in 1933; schoolchildren were taken by their teachers to watch, and it fell neatly across the river, breaking in two places in mid-air. The local Boy Scouts were given the bricks which they themselves retrieved from the river; they were conveyed to the Dawson Road playing field where they were used in the construction of the Scout Hut that still stands there.

48. The buildings which cluster round the tall, stepped chimney are all part of Ullathorne's mill which opened in 1760 and closed in 1932. It manufactured shoe threads and twines, and was owned by an international company with branches in Paris, Melbourne, Brisbane, and Wellington. The local branch was on the Yorkshire side of the river and was officially known as Bridge End Mills. Products included thread for saddlers as well as shoemakers, twines for shopkeepers, and other forms of twine for mattresses and salmon fishing nets. (Some old prints show men fishing with nets and boats in the water below the castle.) It was put to various other uses after its closure as a mill, but is now demolished. The base of the chimney has been retained in its original position, and the rest of the area has been landscaped, giving a striking view of the castle.

R. Tees & Viaduct.

49. This photograph has been taken from one of the windows of the castle and shows the view up the River Tees. The bridge about three quarters of a mile away is the Tees Railway Viaduct, the subject of a later picture (56). Half a mile below it the river was later crossed by the aqueduct of the Stockton and Middlesbrough Water Board; it was built in 1893 so this picture must be older. The river is in flood and sweeps over the weir (known as the 'warren') which normally diverted water towards sluice gates and the mill race on the south bank, from which it drove the machinery of Ullathorne's mill. Floods were more common than they are now, when reservoirs have lessened or regulated the flow both of tributaries and the Tees itself.

*View from Tower, Barnard Castle*

50. This interesting view contrasts in various ways with the preceding picture of the river seen from the castle. This one is from a higher viewpoint, the top of the Baliol tower. The Stockton and Middlesbrough (later 'Tees Valley') Waterboard's aqueduct has been built conveying water to towns over thirty miles away from the reservoir in Baldersdale. The two pipes (a third was added later) are boarded over and pedestrians are allowed to use the bridge. The water level in this picture is low and the weir is retaining the main flow of the river. The long low-roofed shed on the left contains flax, and other paler-coloured lines indicate where more flax is drying in the open air. The field was part of Ullathorne's Mill. Today houses have been built there, and their postal address is 'Flaxfield'. The picture is from a coloured postcard dated 27th December 1907.

The Castle.

51. During the Rising of the North (1569), the castle succumbed to a seige, having withstood the rebel forces of the Neville and the Percy families for a valuable period of eleven days during which the forces supporting Queen Elizabeth were successfully rallied. In the next century much of the castle was dismantled, the stones being used elsewhere, and the building fell into decay. In the nineteenth century a hermit lived alone there and acted as a guide to visitors. According to one story, however, he was evicted for pretending to be a ghost and frightening visitors away. Later, the area depicted was often used for pageants, concerts and dances, especially at Whitsuntide – a tradition still upheld but in another part of the grounds. Now in the care of the Ministry of Works, the castle has lost its naturalised appearance, but interesting historical discoveries have been made.

*Barnard Castle from River*

52. Views of the castle seen from the River Tees were a favourite subject for painters and engravers of the eighteenth and nineteenth centuries, and are among the commonest of scenes chosen by the makers of picture postcards of the town. This one was posted in the 1920's by a member of a Tyneside family, who was 'having a jolly good time at Barney'; she adds that 'the bairns are enjoying themselves up to the mark' and have been in the woods. On the bottom right-hand corner of the picture is a small portion of the weir which is connected to Ullathorne's Mill, and some of the mill's buildings obscure the arch of the Yorkshire side of the County Bridge. The castle dominates the scene, but has to share its cliff with some of the houses which rise from Bridgegate.

53. The great frost of February 1929, was said to be the most severe for the past thirty-five years and it followed a succession of mild winters. Skating was possible on the Tees below and above the Water Bridge from which this picture was taken. At times several hundred people skated, slid, played impromptu ice-hockey or simply promenaded on the ice. Skating also took place on the Greta at Bowes, on Lartington High Pond and at Raby, by invitation of Lord Barnard. There was a harsher side to the long frost: several people were injured on the ice and in Barnard Castle and Startforth over five hundred water pipes burst. In fact a water shortage occurred as frozen springs ceased to flow into the town's reservoir, and the domestic water supply was turned off each night.

54. This rare picture was taken by E. Yeoman, a noted local photographer. It shows the stepping stones at the ford which crosses Percy Beck fifty yards before it joins the Tees. It is taken from the edge of a grassy clearing known as the Band Field. A visitor's description of the scene, from the far bank of the Tees, was published in 1909: *Our ears are beguiled with the strains of music. It is the town's band playing in the delightful shade of 'the greenwood tree'. The music continues to float across to us, and we note the kaleidoscope-like effect made by many figures, young men and maidens, variously garbed, passing to and fro over the Percy Beck, which emerges sparkling from the sylvan shades. The stage and its setting struck us as incomparably beautiful.*

Barnard Castle Woods.

FRITH
82508

55. 'The woods' are still one of Barnard Castle's glories, but this particular grove of trees has gone, felled during the 1960's; though the scene has lost its stateliness, it is still attractive, with younger trees which were planted soon afterwards. Flatts Woods run beside the Tees, but this section follows the course of Percy Beck. In the mid-nineteenth century a Dr. George Edwards designed additional paths to augment the old routes which ran through the wood. The woods belong to Lord Barnard, but by his amiable arrangement with the local council the public, both residents and visitors, have long enjoyed free access. This particular path and bridge seem to have been added to create a pleasing pedestrian route to the former railway station.

Viaduct, Barnard Castle.

56. The Tees Viaduct carried over the river valley the line which led from Barnard Castle to Tebay. This line was opened on 4th July, 1861. Seven years later another line, which also used this viaduct, was opened to connect Middleton-in-Teesdale to Barnard Castle. The viaduct, which cost the North Eastern Railway Company (later L.N.E.R.) £25,119, crossed the Tees at a height of 132 feet. It was a graceful as well as impressive structure and a writer of a local guide book reminded walkers enjoying the riverside scenery to pay tribute to *the engineers whose skill and taste fitted so well their utilitarian masterpiece into a natural setting.* The last train crossed the viaduct in 1965. This card, posted in 1911, shows a lady enjoying the scene under the protection of her parasol.

DEEPDALE, TARTINGTON.

57. After crossing the Tees and parting company with the Middleton line, the route to Kirkby Stephen and Tebay went over Deepdale, by means of the Deepdale Viaduct, known locally as Cat Castle Viaduct. The line crossed Stainmore at a maximum height of 1,370 feet above sea level, and commonly two engines were needed to convey the train over the Pennines. From vantage points in the town, two columns of smoke could be seen as a train crossed the viaduct; this was partly because only small engines could be used owing to severe weight restrictions on two viaducts of which Deepdale was one. Completed in 1858, it was built entirely of iron except for the stone bases and the supports at each end; it crossed the valley in a gentle curve, 740 feet long and 161 feet above the stream.

58. Deepdale Beck runs into the Tees at Barnard Castle. In its lower reaches the level land at the bottom of the valley has at various times been used as a rifle range. The Teesdale Volunteer Infantry, raised about 1803-1809 as Home Defence against Napoleon, used the range under their commander J.B.S. Morritt of Rokeby Hall. 'The Teesdale Poet', Richard Watson (1833-1891), praised the Teesdale Rifle Volunteers in two poems, mentioning that he watched their skill in Deepdale. This postcard, by J.H. Skipper (circa 1913), shows the 3rd D.L.I. at practice there. The range was used in the First World War, fell into disuse, and was revived in the Second World War as a firing range and assault course. Ordnance Survey maps between the wars show six firing points at intervals of a hundred yards.

Deerbolt Camp, Barnard Castle

59. Deepdale forms part of the boundary of 'Deerbolt Park' where some local inhabitants can remember meticulously arranged white tents appearing when members of the Militia held their annual summer training camp. This postcard was posted in 1907. During the Second World War a large brick-built camp was created on the site with parade ground, gymnasium and theatre, and all residential facilities. Members of the Royal Armoured Corps were stationed there. These soldiers and others in nearby camps made a great contribution to the life of the town; among their number, for example, were first class cricketers who played on the town ground, and excellent plays were presented at Deerbolt camp where one of the actors, John le Mesurier, has since become famous as Sgt. Wilson in 'Dad's Army' on television. After extensive rebuilding, a modern Borstal, opened in 1973, now stands on the site.

60. The western limits of the town form the background to a parade on Deerbolt Camp field on the occasion of Queen Victoria's Diamond Jubilee, 1897. Raby Avenue and the adjoining streets are not yet built, but the allotments on the slope are already being cultivated. The cottage of the gamekeeper who looked after Flatts Woods stands out clearly (left centre). Across the fields behind it are the railway goods station buildings, and on the horizon Montalbo Terrace, built on Station Road, shows that the town has begun to reach out to its passenger station. The soldiers are in red tunics with white collars and cuffs; officers wear spiked helmets, and other ranks are in 'Glengarries'. Lt. Colonel R.B. Wilson, mounted, died of illness while serving in the South African War, four years later.

BIRD'S EYE VIEW OF BARNARD CASTLE

61. To gain a bird's eye view of the eastern limits of the town, the photographer climbed to the top of the tower of the Parish Church, and looked along Newgate where the trees that now adorn it had not yet been planted. The Primitive Methodist Church in the foreground was built in 1887; accommodating four hundred people, with schoolroom and vestry adjoining, the whole building and the site cost £2,000. The most distant building on the left is the Barracks, Headquarters of the 1st South Durham Militia (later the 3rd Bn. D.L.I.) from 1864 to 1930. The buildings were then sold to the Urban District Council and divided into dwellings for Council tenants. A system of flatlets for elderly people now stands on the site; the old parade ground is retained as a grassy space and the original impressive gateway still stands with the names and dates of past Commanding Officers.

62. Members of the 'chorus of ancestors' from Gilbert and Sullivan's 'Ruddigore' pose outside the stage door of the Victoria Hall (in a large yard off Newgate) where Barnard Castle Amateur Operatic Society – with the help of some principal performers from other northern societies – performed the Savoy Opera for five successive nights in 1926. It was one of the big events of the year in Teesdale, and a late train ran to Middleton, stopping at intermediate stations, after the Saturday performance. The producer (in evening dress) was Mr. McIntyre, manager of the Darlington Hippodrome, and the scenery and costumes were hired. The theatre had limited dressing accommodation and sometimes the men's chorus dressed in the Rifle Club's shooting range, visible in the background. Visiting principals and some of the ladies' chorus used neighbouring houses.

63. Members of the 17th D.L.I. marched 'at ease' through Newgate in 1915 on their way to camp. The Battalion, which had been formed in the previous October, did not serve overseas as a unit but did train men for other, fighting, battalions. The term 'Kitcheners' came from the English General, 1st Earl Kitchener of Khartoum. He was Secretary of War, 1914-1916, and his face became familiar on recruiting posters with the slogan 'Your country needs you'. Among the horse-drawn vehicles, let down on their shafts while the horses are stabled elsewhere, a motor car strikes a prophetic note for a car sales and repair business has replaced the buildings beside which it was parked. The barrel in the left foreground will remind some inhabitants of one of Newgate's several vanished shops.

64. The Watson family of Spring Lodge (farther along Newgate) has long played a leading part in the life of the town. In this photograph three generations stand on the steps of their house in 1913. William James Watson (1838-1920) stands on the right. Like his two descendants he was a member of the Local Board of Health (or Urban District Council) and the governing bodies of many other local organisations, as well as being Vicar's and People's Warden of the Parish Church. His son, Harry Crawford Watson (1864-1934), standing beside him, joined the volunteer Corps early in life and became Colonel of the 6th D.L.I. which he commanded in the Great War; he strongly supported local sporting and musical organisations. In front stands William Innes Watson who still lives in Spring Lodge; he has fully maintained the family tradition of public service and leadership and is now Deputy Lieutenant of the County.

65. In about 1898, in the time of Mrs. W. Watson, some of the domestic staff of Spring Lodge pose in the garden. Sitting is the cook-housekeeper with the parlourmaid and housemaid; the gardener stands behind. The picture gives only a suggestion of the charm and scope of the grounds. Spring Lodge (the area was well supplied with springs) predated the other buildings at the eastern edge of the town. It was built in 1825 (the architect was possibly Ignatius Bonomi) by William Watson (1794-1883). He was an outstanding local figure, Chairman of the Local Board of Health for thirty consecutive years, and donor of the chiming clock in St. Mary's tower. His eldest son, William James Watson, was an enthusiastic rose-grower and enlarged the grounds, re-arranging them to some extent. In his obituary, 'The Teesdale Mercury' referred to the house and gardens as 'a lovely retreat'.

66. On Friday afternoon, March 30th, 1917, a two-seater reconnaissance bi-plane landed on the Demesnes while on a flight from Glasgow to the South of England. The occasion aroused much interest, and though the picture suggests that the photographer himself has organised the crowd to show the pilot standing by his plane, it was clear that some official supervision was necessary to prevent damage to the aircraft. The Volunteer Training Corps was therefore called upon to keep discipline. Private J.G. Harris was the first guard on duty. Among the young (and not-so-young) spectators, present day readers may recognise Mr. Frank Duffy (front row third from right) and Mr. Frank V. Deacon (fifth from right), who kindly supplied the photograph.

AEROPLANE AT BARNARD CASTLE V.T.C. ON GUARD 31-3-1917

67. Thanks to the V.T.C. we have an excellent view of the plane, which had remained overnight near the wall of the grounds of Spring Lodge. It is a B.E. 2e, the most prolifically produced of the many B.E. variants from the Royal Aircraft Factory at Farnborough. The 2e entered service with the Royal Flying Corps in July 1916, during the Battle of the Somme, and flew in eastern theatres of war. Some were retained for Home Defence duties. A large crowd witnessed the plane take off from the Demesnes at 10.30 on the Saturday morning. It was lucky to have clear weather, for during the Saturday night there was a heavy fall of snow.

68. The construction of a residence for John Bowes and his wife, the Countess of Montalbo, began in 1869. As well as being their home, the building was designed to house their large and growing collection of pictures and other 'objects of art'. The Countess died in 1874 and her husband in 1885. He left £140,000 to maintain his mansion as 'The Bowes Museum' which, with its park, was opened to the public in 1892. This view shows the museum in its early days, much as it looks now; in 1912 a bandstand was added which stood in a direct line between the main gates and the front door of the building, but it has since been removed. The beautiful gates, flanked by appropriately styled lamps (the present-day ones are a replacement of the originals) led to a double carriage-sweep. They are here approached by a ramp of earth because of the curiously low level of the road surface.

69. The Bowes Museum Park is seen here shortly after the Great War. The park occupied what had formerly been twelve fields and a large garden, and the sloping land was adapted to provide a level ornamental area rising steeply towards the surrounding lawns and wooded areas. The central area and the slopes were lavishly planted with flowers, and pillar roses climbed up rustic frames. The Museum itself became justly famous and the park was a popular place in which to stroll or sit and listen to the music of visiting bands which, in 1914, included the Royal Marines (Portsmouth) and the Cameron Highlanders, as well as more local musicians. A stone bandstand had been designed, but the Trustees of the Museum and Park rejected it as too expensive, and the one opened by Lady Glamis in 1912 was a cast-iron structure, surrounded by flowers and with more flowering plants on baskets suspended from its frame.

70. John Bowes' museum was an immense success and is now of international significance, but his own satisfaction was marred by grief at the death of his wife. She had wanted to have a Roman Catholic Chapel in the grounds, expecting one day to be buried in it, and in 1875 John Bowes began the building, to the east of the museum, in loyalty to her memory, but it was not finished in his lifetime. In 1926 stones from the partly-built structure were conveyed by a light railway to a site at the corner of Newgate and Birch Road, to be used in building a Roman Catholic Church for public use. John Bowes and his wife had been interred in Gibside, near Gateshead, but in July 1928, their bodies were re-interred behind the new church, which was consecrated on September 29th, the day on which this photograph was taken.

71. The Museum Park has been the setting for a variety of ceremonial occasions. On 6th July, 1910, the foundation stone of the chapel of the North Eastern County School was laid. The following is an extract from R.C. Hitchcock's history of the school's first fifty years: *Lord Barnard who was both chairman of the Chapel Committee and also Grand Master of the Freemasons of Durham... was able to lay the stone with the ancient ritual of the Order. A procession of 300 Freemasons from Durham, Northumberland and the North Riding was formed in the grounds of the Bowes Museum, and clothed in their regalia (and headed by the Officers Training Corps of the school and the band of the Durham Light Infantry) they proceeded from there to the school. The Lord Bishop of Durham, the Headmaster and others awaited their arrival at the stone.*

72. The North Eastern County School was founded in 1883, but it was temporarily situated in Middleton-one-Row while its Barnard Castle buildings were being constructed. This photograph shows the buildings as the first phase was completed, in 1885-1886, before any trees were planted or the boundary fence constructed. On 19th January 1886, the school was opened for the public to see the premises, and for several hours a steady stream of inhabitants of the town filed through the main rooms. The building consisted of a big schoolroom for assemblies, a dining hall, six classrooms, twelve dormitories, masters' sitting rooms and bedrooms, and a domestic area which included kitchens, a bakery and a steam laundry; the headmaster's house is on the right. On 2nd February the school assembled in the new buildings. There were 116 boarders and 12 day boys. In 1924 the school's name was changed to Barnard Castle School.

73. The Abbey Bridge, crossing the Tees to the east of the town, was provided by J.B.S. Morritt of Rokeby Hall, and opened with Masonic ceremony in 1773. On the Yorkshire side was a toll cottage in two parts — living-room to the left of the road and bedroom to the right. The buildings were demolished in 1958, two years after the last inhabitants left. As well as receiving tolls, the tenants sold postcards and refreshments. Iron gates and railings had formerly enabled them to close the road to either vehicles or pedestrians. A notice-board listed tolls as: Chaise with 2 horses 9d, Gig or dogcart 6d, Wagon with 3 horses 10d, Cattle, per score 1s. 3d, Sheep, per score 8d, Foot Passengers ½d and Motorcars 6d.

74. The Abbey Bridge is here seen on a festive occasion during the Whitsuntide Meet of 1911. On the Sunday morning the cycle clubs rode to Rokeby to enjoy the scenery, and this particular year were delighted by the flowers and trees along Brignal Banks by the River Greta. The Abbey Bridge was a natural stopping place on such outings and this photograph may record the occasion. Another of the annual traditions was that the Past President handed over to his successor a gilt-enamel chain, mounted on a velvet collar, with medallions representing successive Meets. (This was the thirty-fifth.) Here one of the Presidents is wearing the collar; his wife and her friends are in the carriage behind him. Presumably special arrangements were made for paying the tolls; the occupants of the vehicles that have halted on the bridge may have had their own opinions of the festivities!

75. Mr. George H. Maude (1891-1957) was a pioneer in linking Barnard Castle with its surrounding area, especially in the North Riding of Yorkshire. He founded the bus route to Newsham (1912), to Richmond via the upland villages (1928), and to Bowes. He provided transport which linked Scargill and Langleydale to Barnard Castle on Market Days. With his generous and jovial nature, Mr. Maude gave much to local communities in other ways, organising concerts which helped to raise funds for children's annual outings to the sea; he presented the Maude Cup for competition among village cricket teams, was President of the Town Band, and an Urban District Councillor. Here he sits on the bumper bars of one of his early vehicles on the Richmond via Kirkby Hill run, one of the routes by which he brought greater variety to rural life and increased trade to market towns.

76. Towards the end of the nineteenth century an astonishing succession of buildings began to alter the whole character of the Westwick Road. The creation of the huge mansion, which was to be the Bowes Museum, began to rise in the 1870's. Immediately to the east, the North Eastern County School opened its new buildings in 1886, and in 1889 Mr. Blackett of the Sunderland firm of drapers, bought the next piece of land for his country residence, which later became a girls' school, before becoming the Preparatory School for the 'County' School in 1914. The school also expanded its original frontage by adding a sanitorium and an isolation hospital for infectious diseases in 1890. This photograph was probably taken soon afterwards. Along the winding rural road, a lad wanders towards the changed horizon of a changing world.